What Reviewers Say About Dan's Novels

"Dan Walsh is an artist who paints with words. His canvas is the novel, where he uses different colors and hues of words to create a masterpiece." — *New York Journal of Books*

"With a gift for pulling the heartstrings and encouraging a slow build of tears within his reader, Dan Walsh is quickly becoming one of my favorite go-to storytellers." — *USA Today*

"When I'm in the mood for a heartfelt and moving book, I know Dan Walsh always delivers." — *FIRST for Women Magazine*

Other Books by Dan Walsh

Novels – Revell

The Unfinished Gift
The Homecoming
The Deepest Waters
Remembering Christmas
The Discovery
The Reunion
The Dance (with Gary Smalley)
The Promise (with Gary Smalley)
The Desire (with Gary Smalley)
The Legacy (with Gary Smalley)
What Follows After
Keeping Christmas

Novel – Guideposts

Autumn Light (Book 5 – Miracles of Marble Cove)

Novel – Bainbridge Press

When Night Comes (Book 1 – Jack Turner series)

Perfect Peace

in

Imperfect Times

Dan Walsh

To my wife, Cindi, whose example and steady walk with the Lord provokes and inspires me every day, and to my pastor and friend, Ray Dubois, whose care, friendship and advice has made such a difference in my life.

Contents

Introduction

For years, I've been keeping a journal during my quiet times. I don't do it every day, but when a Scriptural theme stirs inside me and captivates my attention in a special way, I write it down. Writing things down often helps me think more clearly. What do I journal about? Mostly things that help me trust God more and live more aware of His presence in my life.

And about things that help me not to worry.

Now, I don't worry about everything. When I do, it's usually about the uncertain things going on in my life. Can you relate? Perhaps you are aware of a lack of peace in your soul right now. Maybe something is troubling you, making you feel restless or unsettled. Just thinking about it can rob you of joy.

I'm talking about things like unanswered questions. Unanswered prayers. Or prayers that were answered, but it seemed like the wrong answer. You don't know why God did what He did or allowed something unpleasant to happen.

You try not to think about these things, try all sorts of things to blot them out. But they keep popping back up. When you do something to alleviate the stress, it doesn't last very long. The fretting thoughts are right there to greet you when you're done. Why is that?

I think it's because, deep inside, we know that these things that unsettle us are real. They aren't figments of our imagination. Life really is hard at times and often full of uncertainty. The longer we live, the more obvious this becomes. We don't feel in control, because, well…we're not.

Too many unplanned things have happened. Too many unwanted surprises. Things we worked hard for did not happen; other things we never wanted to happen happened instead. This didn't just occur once or on rare occasions. But several times. And if you're old enough, maybe more times than you can count.

Each time we experience a life ambush, we become more aware of how little control we have. So we worry…and fret. About the uncertain things going on in our lives now, or the things that may come after that. Even when things are going well, we worry about what might bring these good days to an end.

You've probably heard that the Bible is full of God's promises. Here's one of them: **This life will be filled with trouble.** I'm paraphrasing here, but a dozen verses that say this just popped into my head. Jesus said something just like this at the Last Supper in John 16:23. The truth is, we can't avoid the problems and trials in life any more than we can dodge raindrops running through a parking lot. Trouble-free living is not what the Bible offers.

But at the Last Supper, Jesus followed that promise of trouble with this: "*Be of good cheer, for I have overcome the world.*" The Bible may promise a life filled with trouble, but it also promises that it is possible to live our lives filled with joy, peace and freedom from worry.

How? Well, we need a little help. We can't get there on our own.

Left to ourselves, we drift easily into worrying and fretting about everything. This leads us into even more trouble. When we're anxious, we'll do things that make our situation worse, and make us feel worse about our situation.

Experiencing this promised joy and peace doesn't come automatically. There's something we must do. A choice we must make. A verse in Isaiah explains what that choice is. It is a path to true peace in this life.

A Perfect Peace.

> "*You will keep Him in **perfect peace**, whose mind is **stayed on you**. Because he trusts you.*" (Isa. 26:3, ESV)

That's what this little book is about. Learning this secret. Not just in our heads, but also in our hearts. How to keep our minds "stayed on Him" and, in those times when our mind wanders, how to find our way back quickly. It's a kind of peace the world cannot give and cannot take away. It costs us nothing, but it cost Jesus everything. And because He paid that price this peace is always available to every Christian, at every moment of the day.

But having this information is not the same as living in the good of it, day after day, week after week. So day after day, week after week for the next month or so, we're going to look intently at this truth of God, this promise God holds out to us.

A promise of Perfect Peace.

The goal will be to apprehend it, to own it, to develop new habits that will help us keep our minds "stayed on Him."

Day 1

The Foundation of True Peace

Before we look into the practical things God's Word says about experiencing His peace, let's make sure we're all standing on a firm foundation. What is necessary to experience peace at a foundational level, and why do many Christians fail to experience it?

The desire for peace is a universal thing, isn't it? Everyone wants peace in their personal life and in the world, right? Well, it can't be everybody or we'd have it already, wouldn't we?

I grew up in the sixties, during the height of the Vietnam War. I vividly remember thousands of protestors fighting with hundreds of policemen in riot gear, holding up signs that cried out for peace. Think of the irony: thousands of people screaming, swearing, punching, throwing rocks, breaking windows, being injured and injuring others in an effort to bring about world peace.

I read an article by a military general who said in the seven-thousand years of recorded history, man has only known peace on earth 5 percent of the time. Isn't that amazing...and sad? Just in the last century, we've seen World War I, World War II, the Korean War, the

Vietnam War, the Cold War, the War in Iraq and Afghanistan, not to mention the dozens of wars and conflicts going on in other parts of the world.

The truth is, the only thing required for wars to keep popping up and for relational conflicts between people to keep occurring is for people to keep being born. That's it. Here's the equation:

Keep having babies = No peace on earth.

Everyone knows those cute, almost angelic little beings we bring home from the hospital will turn on their parents and start demanding their own way, often before their first birthday. It happens without exception. Doesn't matter if they're a boy or girl, born here or in any other country, or any other culture around the world. Children will rebel against anyone who tries to tell them what to do, even if it's for their own good.

Why is this true? And why is it without exception?

The Bible tells us plainly. We are all born in a condition called "sin." What is Sin? It is that internal force that causes us to go our own way, to do our own thing. In Isaiah 53:6, it says: "*All we like sheep have gone astray; we have turned, every one, to his own way*" (ESV).

This is why we have no peace. The foundation is missing. True peace can come to us only when we enter into peace with God. The very next line in Isaiah 53 says: "*And the Lord has laid on Him the iniquity (sin) of us all.*"

The prophet is referring to Christ and what He did on the cross. Jesus came, sent by His Father, free from the contamination of sin (that's what the virgin birth is all about). He lived His entire life obeying all of God's commands and resisting every temptation, so that He might become a perfect sacrifice for our sin. He then offered Himself on the cross, so that the punishment we deserve for all our sins—all our moments of selfishness and disobedience—could be poured out on Jesus instead of on us.

This, my friends, is true love. God's love. Redeeming Love. Receiving Jesus Christ as Lord and Savior is the foundation of true peace. We can never expect to have peace in our hearts or with others until we first experience peace with God.

If you've never experienced this peace or received Christ as your Lord and Savior, but you believe everything I have just said, you can pray to receive Him now.

Lord Jesus, thank You for dying on the cross to pay the price for my sins, for all the times I have done my own thing and gone my own way. Today, I turn control of my life over to You. Please come into my heart and make it Your own. I want to experience the peace of God and to walk with You, as your child, from now on. Thank you for saving me and for making it possible for me to be adopted into Your family. In Jesus' name, Amen.

Day 2
True Peace is a Person

True Peace is a Person?

I've already talked about *what* Perfect Peace is. The secret is found in this Scripture (and in dozens more like it, which we'll meditate on in future chapters):

> "*You will keep him **in perfect peace**, whose mind is stayed on You, because he trusts in You.*" (Isaiah 26:3, ESV)

Do you see the promise here? What is being offered to us? Perfect Peace. Do you also see what this perfect peace hinges on? What makes it possible?

"*You* will keep him…"

"…whose mind is stayed on *You*…"

"…because he trusts in *You*."

Perfect Peace is not simply the absence of trouble in one's life. It's found in a close relationship with a Person. The Scriptures tell us this Person is Jesus Christ. He is called the Prince of Peace (Isa. 9:6). We're told Jesus is, "*the radiance of the glory of God and the exact imprint of his nature*" (Heb 1:3, ESV). Jesus is the "You" Isaiah is talking about. Perfect Peace comes to those who keep their minds "stayed" (focused or fixed) on Christ.

This involves a bit more than simply becoming a Christian. If Perfect Peace came automatically when people come to Christ, Christians would never worry or fear, never fret or become anxious.

But they do.

If you're like me, you've known moments of real peace. Moments when you've trusted God fully for your life, for everything going on in your life. And in those moments, you knew real peace. The problem is the word "moments."

The moments didn't last.

The promise of Isaiah 26:3 is not to have moments of peace in our lives. The promise is that God would "*keep us in Perfect Peace.*" So why is it that most of us only know moments of peace?

I believe the problem stems from our embedded tendency to live independently from God. We aren't convinced we need God as much as we do.

What did Adam and Eve do right after The Fall? They hid from God and tried to fix the problem themselves. This is what we all try to do. We'd prefer it if God would make this perfect peace something we receive once, then it stays with us the rest of our lives, regardless of how close we live to God, day to day.

But that's not how it works.

You probably already know this (it's why you're reading this book). The perfect peace Isaiah is referring to is given to those who draw near to God *each day* and stay near to God *throughout the day*. It is directly connected to the level of relationship we maintain with Jesus Christ.

God will keep us in perfect peace when our minds are stayed on Him, on Jesus. Jesus enjoyed this peace and experienced it every day on earth, because He kept His mind stayed on His Father. He wants us to enjoy this same level of peace as we keep our minds stayed on Him.

To help us experience this fully, Jesus gives us a wonderful gift. The gift of Himself, in the presence of the Holy Spirit. We'll look more into this in Day Three.

Lord, thank You for giving Your life to make it possible for me to experience Your Perfect Peace. And for living now within me, so I can experience this peace every day. I want my relationship with You to increase. I want my dependence on You to increase, and my awareness of Your Presence at work in my life. Help me to keep my mind stayed on You today, and to trust You for everything I face. In Jesus' name, Amen.

Day 3

The Holy Spirit's Role

As we've already learned, you can be a Christian and not enjoy Perfect Peace. But this peace is something God *intends* for us to experience. To help us, He provides the most wonderful gift. The gift of Himself. I'm referring to the gift of the Holy Spirit, the third Person of the Trinity.

Jesus introduced His disciples to the Holy Spirit at the Last Supper. John's Gospel tells us the most about this, so let's turn there.

> "*I am the vine, you are the branches.*" (John 15:5, NIV)

This is a familiar passage to many of us, said at the Last Supper, and a powerful metaphor. Because it is familiar, we can sometimes forget what was happening at the time Jesus said it. **It was the eve of His death**. After three years of being with His disciples, Jesus was about to leave them. Not just for a short journey; He was about to die a violent death at the hands of His enemies.

Yet here, Jesus shares this picture where He is the vine and they are the branches. The meaning is clear: *They were*

11

to live in complete dependence upon Him. But how could they? He was leaving them that very night.

It made more sense when Jesus broke the bread and wine and said, "Remember Me whenever you do this." Those sound like words you'd say when you're going away.

But with this vine metaphor, Jesus isn't speaking of remembering Him. He's talking about *an ongoing relationship* with Him that extends well beyond the horrific events of this night. It must have been confusing for the disciples to consider how such a dependent relationship with Christ could even be possible, since He was about to die and return to heaven.

A few moments later He explains exactly *how* it would become possible. **The Holy Spirit would come.** He had been with Jesus from the beginning. His Presence and fellowship united Jesus to His Father while He was on earth. Jesus talked about the Holy Spirit **six times that night** (more than any other theme).

The first time, Jesus said: "*…And I will ask the Father, and He will give you another Advocate, who will never leave you. He is the Holy Spirit, who leads into all truth.*" (John 14:15-17). Jesus identifies the Holy Spirit as the "Spirit of truth." And to offset the sad news about His departure, Jesus says, He *"will never leave you."*

In the very next verse, Jesus adds: "*I will not leave you as orphans; I will come to you.*" He doesn't mean physically, He means through the Holy Spirit. The Spirit will serve as a living link to Jesus for us.

And that's what happened. In the Book of Acts and Paul's epistles, we see them constantly talking about the Holy Spirit. It's very evident…**they related to the Spirit in a personal and dependent way.**

Okay, so they did. The question is…do we?

I don't think so. I think many of us relate to a different "functional Trinity," than the Father, Son and Holy Spirit.

We depend on other things or other people in a way God intended us to depend upon the Holy Spirit. Like the Church, or the Bible, or our Pastor. Certainly, these other things are important. But they are not the Vine and cannot give us life and peace. They are a means God uses to help us. But we must learn to depend on the primary "Helper" Jesus talked about at the Last Supper.

The Holy Spirit.

Lord, thank You for giving us, for giving me, the Holy Spirit. Because He lives in me now, You and the Father are always with me. Even when there is no one around, I am never alone anymore. Help me today, and in the days to come, to grow in my awareness and dependence of this precious gift. The gift of Yourself in the presence of the Spirit. In Jesus' name, Amen.

Day 4
God's Timing

Almost every believer struggles to some extent (some to a great extent) with the timing of God. If we're honest, most of us would say God moves a little too slowly for us.

But things are not as they seem:

> *"For my thoughts are not your thoughts, neither are your ways my ways, declares the LORD. For as the heavens are higher than the earth, so are my ways higher than your ways and my thoughts than your thoughts."* (Isaiah 55:8-9, ESV)

People who worry about the uncertainties in their life often have this in common: **they have lots of thoughts.** Consider your present situation (the one you're always thinking about). How many thoughts have you had about it so far? Dozens, hundreds?

As I've sought to become more dependent on God, I've discovered a basic problem, an inner conflict between that desire and the way I sometimes behave. Somewhere along the line I became a person who thinks way too much.

Hours in thought, minutes in prayer.

During a trial, the sheer volume of thoughts I'd pile up trying to figure out a solution reveals whose mind and thoughts I trust in the most. Mine. But I also realized, some of my problems were too big to think my way out of. And many of the solutions I came up with just made matters worse.

God also has thoughts, many thoughts, about the situations that perplex us. His thoughts and His ways (what He does with His thoughts) aren't just a little different than ours. Isaiah says, they aren't the same at all. We don't think or do things the way God does.

Here's why: God's thoughts and ways are *infinitely higher* than ours. The gap between our ideas and His are as high as the heavens are above the earth. That's no small gap.

God feels no stress as He manages the wonders of a universe. I feel stress as I ponder an unpaid bill. As I considered this gap between God's wisdom and mine, I realized why I often preferred my own thoughts and ideas to God's.

God's ways seem much slower than mine.

Whatever my situation, I can usually think of a handful of things that, if done right away, would fix my problem. If I were God, I'd do those few things right now.

But that's not what happens.

I don't have the power to pull off what I'm thinking and God refuses to cooperate. So my problem continues, far longer than I think it should. I do pray. But then I begin looking for an instant breakthrough. When it doesn't come, I'm tempted to stop praying and start thinking some more.

Once as I prayed and pondered this passage, I began to reflect on God's apparent slowness. I realized that God's ways seem slower, because He takes all the necessary details into account in His solutions. I may think of three things that need to happen, but God sees thirty things (or three-hundred things).

God's plan only seems slower because God is infinitely wise—and we are not. When I look back at other situations God has rescued me from, I can see His wisdom vindicated. I see dozens of things God caused or allowed to happen—things I never considered—that resulted in just the right solution to my dilemma.

Here's a prayer to help get our thoughts more in sync with His:

Lord, today I defer to Your wisdom and thank You for the evidences of grace already visible in my situation. I thank You for the promises in Your Word and Your abounding patience toward me. And for all the testimonies of past situations where Your faithfulness has passed every test. Help me to trust You fully in this new situation and release it completely into Your capable hands. Help me to pray more about this throughout the day, and think less. In Jesus' name, Amen.

Day 5

Trust God…Really?

The namesake verse for this book has been Isaiah 26:3, which promises "perfect peace" to those whose minds are stayed (fixed) on God. It ends with this phrase: "…*because he trusts in you.*"

That's our topic today.

Let's begin with a familiar passage about Trust.

> *"Trust in the Lord with all your heart, and do not lean on your own understanding. In all your ways acknowledge him, and he will make straight your paths."* — (Prov. 3:5-6, ESV)

This may be the first Bible verse I ever memorized (over forty years ago). And yet, it is still one I can struggle to obey. A big part of me genuinely wants to do this. To just let go of the things that concern me and trust God completely.

Part of my struggle is the absolute aspects of this command. Trust in the Lord with ALL your heart. DO NOT lean on your own understanding. What is meant by, *do not lean on my own under-standing*? Simply put, we're being told not to put our trust in the ideas and thoughts we come up with. Instead, we're instructed to trust in the Lord about the situation, whatever it is, fully and completely. Literally, to ask for His help and wisdom and then to turn the situation over to Him.

When we do this, we are no longer the one in charge; we become the follower. The promise offered to us, if we would do this, is that God will sovereignly intervene and make our crooked and confusing paths clear and straight.

I love this idea.

My tendency, however, leans in a different direction. I consider a situation then immediately begin to think of solutions. I come up with Plan A, then spend time thinking about Plan B, in case Plan A fails. I may even think through a Plan C. For the most part, when I do this, I'm even trying to think of biblical solutions.

The snare is…I assume that the plans and ideas I come up with are probably from God. Then I act on them hoping I have God's permission, if not His blessing. The problem is…I can do all this without spending hardly any time seeking God for His direction or surrendering my life to His will.

What I'm really doing here is nothing more than a religious approach to "leaning on my own understanding." I'm not trusting in the Lord with all my heart. I'm like a backseat driver who wants to be in the driver's seat—and thinks he should be. I'm unable to trust that the One actually driving the car can handle the situation without my advice. I'm finding it hard to just sit back and enjoy the ride. My thoughts are on the road ahead, the speedometer, the traffic lights, the crazy drivers on the road all around us.

What this passage calls us to do is to let go completely, to give up control, to let God be completely in charge of our situation. And to *not* lean on—or trust in—our own understanding of things anymore. Read this passage again if you're not sure. Look it up in any translation you'd like. They'll pretty much say the same thing.

That doesn't mean we have no role to play, or no work to do. But our role and how we accomplish it needs to flow out from this foundation of trust.

God want us to trust in Him, first and foremost. To relate to Him, the way Jesus related to the Father. And He promises that when we do, He will intervene personally to direct and supervise our affairs.

Lord, forgive me for treating You as if you don't know what You're doing, as if you're not really able to handle the affairs of my life. You are infinitely wise, almighty in power, and love me with an everlasting love. I relinquish complete control of everything in my life to You today and ask for Your grace to keep doing this all day. Lord, help me change in this area, to seek You first in all my life situations. In Jesus' name, Amen.

Day 6

Tearing Down Imaginary Walls -

Today, I want to look at an often misunderstood passage of Scripture. Here's the verse:

> "*For the weapons of our warfare are not of the flesh but have divine power to destroy strongholds. We destroy arguments and every lofty opinion raised against the knowledge of God, and take every thought captive to obey Christ...*" (2 Cor. 10:4-5, ESV)

I have often seen this passage taught by well-meaning people as if Paul was talking about battling Satan. Certainly, there are biblical texts that speak of fighting the devil, but this isn't one of them. If you read this passage carefully, and consider the verses above and below it, you'll see that the devil is never mentioned. The "strongholds" Paul says we should destroy are *opinions and thoughts* that contradict the truth of God's Word.

God knows that what we *think* about something matters a great deal. Here's the basic principle:

We all live within the boundaries of whatever we

believe, whether that belief is true or false.

If we get to a place where a *thought* or idea graduates into something we *believe*, we will live by that belief as though it were real and true, whether it is true or not. One relevant example is the idea of whether or not God truly loves us.

God's Word says that He does. He loves us with an everlasting love (Ps. 36:5). He loved us enough to send His own Son to die in our place (Eph 5:2). He loves us enough to forgive our sins completely and remove them from His sight (Ps. 103:11-12). He tells us His love is so strong, nothing can ever separate us from it (Rom 8:37-39).

But let's say we fail Him, maybe in a significant way. A thought comes into our mind that says, "*How can God love me now?*" We start thinking that we don't deserve to be loved as much as the Bible teaches, so we shrink back, at first just slightly, from believing God really can—and does—love us that much.

Over time, our sense of God's love erodes further, to where we don't *feel* His love very much, which only strengthens our sense of unworthiness. At that point, our feelings take the highest place in our hearts, displacing the truth of God's Word completely.

We now *believe* God doesn't love us as much as the Bible says. From that point on, we will live within the boundary of a new belief: "*God doesn't love me very much, and why should He?*"

From there, each new failure on our part and each new

disappointment in our circumstances only reinforce this sense of being unloved by God. Each of these moments adds another brick to the wall that makes us feel separated from God's love.

But this passage in 2 Corinthians 10 tells us that this wall of separation, this stronghold, between us and God **is a lie**. We are standing on the other side of a wall that **isn't real**, that does not even exist to God. It's an imaginary wall, a stronghold of our own making, from thoughts that we decided at some point to believe.

This passage (along with countless others like it) brings us wonderful news. God is ready to tear down this wall at this very moment. Not brick by brick over time, but to completely demolish it in one moment like the walls of Jericho.

But we have a part to play. We must reject these "lofty opinions raised against the knowledge of God" and embrace God's thoughts, God's truth, about us, and about His love. This is what it means to "take every thought captive to obey Christ."

Lord, thank You for helping me see these subtle thoughts that I've come to believe that contradict the truth of Your Word. Forgive me for believing them and allowing them to become a stronghold in my life. They have kept me from enjoying the richness of Your love. I now fully accept and believe again the truth of Your Word, that you love me with an everlasting love, and that nothing in all of creation can ever separate me from Your love. In Jesus' name, Amen.

Day 7

The Slippery Slope of Anxious Thoughts

Negative thoughts can be quite powerful if they hit you at just the right time.

Some Christians might consider such thoughts "attacks of the devil," and some might be. Paul gives credibility to this idea in a passage in Ephesians 6. In context, he *is* talking about battling spiritual forces of evil. He uses the metaphor of a soldier starting off his day by putting on all the various pieces of armor he'll need to protect himself. After listing several of these, Paul writes: "*In addition to all of these, hold up the shield of faith* **to stop the fiery arrows of the devil.**" (Eph. 6:16)

These "fiery arrows" could very well be referring to the negative, fearful or condemning thoughts the devil telepathically tosses our way. But I don't believe all negative thoughts come from the devil. We can think ourselves into all kinds of trouble without any help.

Whether these thoughts come from the devil, our own mind or somewhere else, the effect can be the same. A fire left unchecked tends to spread and consume everything in its path. Anxious, negative thoughts can be like that when they hit us in unguarded moments. So, they rob us of joy and peace.

In time, they can grow into a stronghold of anxiety and fear that walls us in and takes us captive.

Once as I prayed through a difficult and uncertain time, the Lord showed me how this pattern of negative thoughts had unfolded in my mind. It was as if I saw the whole thing in slow-motion. This time, I caught onto it quickly. But left to themselves these anxious thoughts can become a slippery slope sliding downward to discouragement. If left long enough, they can lead to depression and fear.

Here's the pattern I saw:

First, I am presented with a situation *I don't like*; one where I don't have *any real control* over the outcome. I begin to think about what this *could mean* or what *could happen* down the road. A number of "what-if" questions begin to stir. Then I start to imagine that what could happen *will* happen.

Now, my emotions and feelings kick into gear. I actually begin to "see" these things in my mind and feel them in my emotions. I start to *become angry* or *give into fear*. Then I think about what action I must take to keep this negative thing from happening.

Sadly, all this can occur in a matter of moments. And none of it is based in reality. All of it is coming from *thoughts* going on inside my head. I've already slid down the slippery slope and don't even know it.

Here's another important thing to consider: None of the thoughts or actions I take from this point are rooted or grounded in faith or love. **So, they can't possibly be inspired by God.**

This thought-pattern is nothing more than the temptation to anxiety, a lack of trust rooted in unbelief. Its intention is to lead me into fear and, possibly, toward some destructive consequences that could flow from the poor choices I make under its influence.

The good news is this time my "shield of faith" functioned properly extinguishing the fiery arrows before they had a chance to do any damage. Understanding Paul's lesson in Ephesians 6, it's clear he is advising us to put on the full armor of God every day (just like any soldier or police officer would do before heading out into dangerous territory).

To me, this imagery speaks of the need for a deliberate time set aside every morning to draw near to God and allow him to strengthen us and equip us to face the day ahead.

Lord, thank You for not leaving me alone, to face this day alone. You are here with me, willing to help me put on Your armor, so that I can face this day in faith and enjoy Your perfect peace. Protect me from the evil one and even from my own thoughts when they lead me astray. Help me to extinguish every one of these thoughts with my shield before they rob me of the joy found in Your presence. In Jesus name, Amen.

Day 8
Orphans No More

Today we're going to look at the Fatherhood of God. Most Christians are familiar with the term. It is rarely used in the Old Testament, but used all the time in the New. Jesus introduced it to us in the gospels and referred to God as Father on a regular basis.

When Jesus' disciples asked Him to teach them how to pray, he starts off with: "Our Father" (...*who art in Heaven, hallowed be Thy name*). Thousands of people who don't even follow the Lord know this prayer.

So, the idea of God as Father is not strange to most of us. But how many of us actually live in the good of this? Live our daily lives enjoying the benefit of God as our Father, the way Jesus did?

I believe the number is quite small. In reality, I think more of us live like *spiritual orphans*. I did, for a long time. And for the most part, when I did I was completely unaware of it. The whole time I referred to God as Father. I believe in the Trinity, and that the first person of the Trinity is...God, the Father.

But Jesus related to God as Father in very real ways. He oriented His entire life and ministry—everything He did, everything He said—to please His Father. We're told He always obeyed His Father's will (John 8:28). And because He did, He experienced one very real and obvious benefit (among others).

Jesus never worried about anything.

He was never afraid. His heart and mind were continually at peace. We never see Jesus fretting about what might happen in the future. We never see Him worrying about provisions, whether His health would hold up. He never worried about what people thought of Him, the bad things they said, or what they might do to Him.

Why? Because Jesus did not live as an orphan, but as the Son of a Heavenly Father who cared for Him day and night. A Father who had the power to care for Him and the commitment to watch over every detail of His life.

It dawned on me some years back, as I read something Jesus said at the Last Supper, that I didn't live like this. In John 14:18, Jesus said: "*I will not leave you as orphans; I will come to you.*"

At that moment, it dawned on me: I lived like an orphan most of the time, not like someone cared for by a loving Father. That's why I struggled with anxiety and worried about so many things. An orphan has no parent in their life they can turn to, no one to direct and guide them, to provide for them, etc. They must fend for themselves. They must think for themselves, solve their own problems, figure out what needs to be done, and do it.

Spiritually, this was how I functioned day-to-day,

evidenced by my lack of prayer and dependence on the Spirit of God. The fact that I at least attempted to live biblically and think of things God might want me to do is not the same as depending on the Lord, or being Spirit-led the way Jesus was. I lived like and worried like an orphan, as one fending for himself.

Can you relate to this?

I'm so thankful God rescued me from this deception. He's replaced it with a strong desire to actually live, day to day, an orphan no more. I want to wake up as Jesus did and immediately turn the affairs of the coming day over to my Heavenly Father (which is really how the Our Father prayer begins).

If you are a Christian, this is your right as a child of God. You, too, are an orphan no more. Jesus wants you to experience the blessing of being cared for at every moment of the day, even when troubles come. What Jesus said to His disciples at the Last Supper, He is saying to you: "I will not leave you as orphans; I will come to you."

Lord, thank You for adopting me into your family, for making me Your own. Forgive me for continuing to live as though that wasn't true. As though I were still an orphan, living life on my own. Give me the grace to stop thinking this way and to start seeing myself, more and more, as Your child. Thank You that this is true not just today, but for eternity. In Jesus name, Amen.

Day 9

Recognizing the Power of Drift

"Drift is always away."

I heard this quote at a pastor's conference many years ago in a message by Christian counselor and author, Dr. David Powlison. He was sharing things he'd learned about how to have an effective personal prayer time, a quiet time. You might think such a message would be unnecessary in a room full of pastors. Not so. Pastors are often very busy people and can struggle, like anyone else, to spend adequate time alone with God.

Powlison was putting his finger on the pulse of a very real hindrance to a healthy devotional life.

The problem of *Drift*.

So let's look at Drift more closely. Here's why we should: *You drift. I drift. All God's people drift.* And we don't just drift occasionally. It's fair to say we are all *prone* to drift. The Bible often uses the metaphor of "sheep" to describe what people are like. The prophet Isaiah said: "*All we like sheep have gone astray. Everyone has turned to his own way*" (Isa. 53:6, ESV).

It's the nature of sheep to stray, to drift. We don't have to intend to, or mean to, or even want to. We just do it.

It's in our nature. Some of you are experiencing drift right now (you're being tempted to drift away from what I'm saying to think of other things). The problem with drift—as Powlison pointed out—drift is always away. That's the direction it takes us. Away from God. And away from what God wants us to focus on. Drift encourages us to turn to our own way instead, to do our own thing.

What Dr. Powlison said next at that pastor's conference was also profound. *"No one drifts into an excellent walk with God. We have to be intentional about it."* He went on to cite one example after another of powerful men and women of God in Christian history who pursued time alone with God; not just occasionally, but every day.

The reason we need to seek God every day is because **the force of drift is with us every single day**, whether we realize it or not. It greets us as soon as we wake up in the morning.

I happen to live in Florida. One thing you see all over the place in my state are boats and docks and marinas. If you drive by a marina in my town you'll see boats of every shape and size.

But there's one thing all of these boats have in common. And because this thing exists, there is one practice every boat owner is completely committed to, something they do every time they pull into the dock, without fail.

They tie the boat up.

Why do they do this? Because they know, **drift is real**. It's a force that exists whether they like it or not. They know exactly what would happen if they neglected to tie their boat up even once. Their boat would begin to drift and, by the next time they returned, it would be gone for good. Can you imagine the nightmare in every harbor if even half the boat owners failed to recognize the reality of drift?

But I think that's exactly what many Christians do. We fail to recognize the reality of drift. I don't any longer. I've accepted it as a fact of life in this fallen world. Recognizing it has kept my motivation pretty high to seek God every day.

For our closing prayer this time, I thought of the lyrics to a hymn I dearly love, **Come Thou Fount of Every Blessing**. Really, just one verse in particular.

Oh to grace, how great a debtor
Daily I'm constrained to be!
Let Thy goodness, like a fetter,
Bind my wandering heart to Thee.
Prone to wander, Lord, I feel it,
Prone to leave the God I love;
Here's my heart, O take and seal it,
Seal it for Thy courts above.

Day 10
Staying In "Today"

One of the most valuable and most challenging things I've been seeking to master in recent years is the idea of living for the Lord one day at a time. My goal is to awaken each day aware of my complete dependence on Him and to quickly yield myself to His control.

The reason is simple. This is how Jesus lived, the way He related to His Father. We never see Jesus wrestling with the "tyranny of the urgent," chained to His calendar or planning book. Some of us may need to plan out certain things as part of our job, but many of us take it so much further, planning out every aspect of our personal lives, sometimes down to the last detail.

Jesus lived very differently. He awakened each day focused on following the will of His Father, wherever that led Him. Whenever Jesus talked to His disciples about time, He said things like: *"Therefore do not worry about tomorrow, for tomorrow will worry about itself. Each day has enough trouble of its own."* (Matt. 6:34).

In the Book of Acts, the disciples' focus seems pretty much the same as Jesus'. Paul's life seems pretty much the same. There are no examples anywhere in Scripture of our modern practice of planning out the details of our lives. No instructions to do this and, certainly, no commands. So why do we do it? Why is it so often the *norm* for us?

Exactly.

Which is why I've started to actively resist thoughts that tempt me to carry tomorrow's burdens today. If I don't, all the unsure and uncertain things in my life rise up to confront me. The problem is, I can't do a single thing about all this extra weight I'm carrying.

Even if I could travel into the future, who's to say I could fix the situation? Or, that what I imagine could happen will happen the way I'm seeing it now? Nothing in the present happens the way I plan. Every week, sometimes every day, surprises come in and mess up my plans. This pattern has been going on my entire life. Why would I think it will be any different in the future?

This kind of planning is not God's best for us. James said:

*Now listen, you who say, "Today or tomorrow we will go to this or that city, spend a year there, carry on business and make money." **Why, you do not even know what will happen tomorrow.** What is your life? You are a mist that appears for a little while and then vanishes. Instead, you ought to say, "If it is the Lord's will, we will live and do this or that."* (James 4:13-15)

We have only this day—TODAY—assured to us. We have no promise of tomorrow, at least not on this earth.

My most important task is to begin each day drawing near to God (Ps. 5:2-3). To surrender my will, my plans, and my agenda to the One who loved me and gave Himself for me (Luke 9:23, Gal 2:20).

God's faithfulness awakens with the sunrise. His mercies are "new every morning" (Lam. 3:22-23). As for our future, all the days of our life, though turning one page at a time for us, are already written in God's book (Ps. 139:16). How many pages do I have left in my book? What things might happen in those pages? I don't know. But this I do know…the One who made me, the One who died and gave His life for me, He knows how many pages I have left and what is written on each one.

And we know He has promised to be with us as each page unfolds, leading us and guiding us by His Spirit, as we yield our will and take hold of His hand.

Lord, help me to learn this new and living way, to stop carrying the weight of tomorrow's troubles and concerns. Thank You for the grace You've provided for today. When tomorrow comes, You will be there, just as present and willing to give me fresh grace to see me through whatever I might face. I ask you to take away any burden You have not asked me to carry, even now. Give me Your rest in its place. In Jesus name, Amen.

Day 11

A Great Place to Be

Sometimes, I don't feel all that confident and assured about the circumstances in my life. Or maybe about the path I'm on, or a decision I've made. I want to be strong and confident. I may even act like I am for a while, but soon realize I'm making more of an effort than how I really feel.

I wasn't always like this. When I was younger, I almost always felt confident and strong. But now as I look back, I think I was fooling myself much of the time. The dictionary has a word for this. It's called *bravado*. It means, *"a pretentious, swaggering display of courage."*

The trials of life, over time, have a way of eroding one's bravado. Now I see it for what it is, and call it what it is.

Weakness.

Which isn't the same as being a weakling or a coward. It's about being honest about how I'm really doing vs. pretending to be something that I'm not.

Here's an example from my writing life. I've written over a dozen novels so far under contract by two major Christian publishers. I've won numerous national writing awards. My novels have received rave reviews in magazines, internet blogs and from hundreds of customers on Amazon. One of my novels is being made into a feature film.

You'd think with a record like that I should feel strong and confident as I set out to write my next book. But I don't. I have doubts about whether I can do it again. What if I can't? What if the well has run dry? What will I do then?

Where does such weakness come from? Did I miss something in my childhood? Have I experienced some traumatic events that have eroded my self-confidence? The answer to both of these questions is yes. But that's not where this sense of weakness comes from.

The real reason, I believe, is actually **a kindness from God**. Not something I should dread, but something to celebrate. God, in His mercy, has lifted the veil of bravado and self-sufficiency I used to walk in, and helped me see my true condition before Him.

Adam and Eve's Fall created the illusion that we can handle everything just fine on our own. By design, we were made to live in a dependent relationship with God. Apart from Him, we have no spiritual strength of our own. This is why we feel weak.

It's not really a feeling. It's absolutely the truth.

But there is good news. God has made the strength we lack continuously available to us, through Christ, and in abundant supply. Of course, we won't benefit from this strength if we continue to walk in the *illusion* of strength. We must learn what Paul learned; that is, to become content with this sense of spiritual weakness. It is the very thing that keeps drawing us near to God to receive a fresh supply of strength.

Listen as Paul shares the revelation God gave him after suffering a difficult trial: "*Three different times I begged the Lord to take it away. Each time he said, 'My grace is all you need. My power works best in weakness.' So now I am glad to boast about my weaknesses, so that the power of Christ can work through me. That's why I take pleasure in my weaknesses, and in the insults, hardships, persecutions, and troubles that I suffer for Christ. For when I am weak, then I am strong.*" (2 Cor. 12:8-10, NLT)

Do you ever feel weak or overwhelmed? Can you see that this is actually **a great place to be**, spiritually speaking? Because now you know it's time to draw near to God to receive His power and strength.

Lord, thank You for opening my eyes to see my true condition before You. I may be weak, but because of Your great mercy, I don't have to pretend to be strong anymore. You are willing to give me all the strength I need to overcome whatever I am going through, or will go through today. Thank You for Your amazing grace. Strengthen me now, I pray. In Jesus' name, Amen.

Day 12
The Decisive Difference

"Listen to me, all who hope for deliverance—all who seek the Lord! Consider the rock from which you were cut, the quarry from which you were mined. Yes, think about Abraham, your ancestor, and Sarah, who gave birth to your nation. Abraham was only one man when I called him. ***But when I blessed him,*** *he became a great nation."* (Isa 51:1-2)

I meditated on this verse during a quiet time, specifically the part that credits the difference in Abraham's life as coming from the blessing of God. Soon, a second verse came to mind:

*"****Unless the Lord builds the house,*** *those who build it labor in vain.* ***Unless the Lord watches over the city,*** *the watchman stays awake in vain."* (Psalm 127:1)

The theme that began to form in my mind as I meditated on both of these passages was:

In every facet of my life, the blessing of God is the decisive difference.

Success according to this world's thinking has nothing to do with God's blessing. Few people spend any time seeking it, expecting it, or even considering whether it matters. Worldly wisdom suggests that success comes from things like diligence, the pursuit of excellence, who you know and perhaps even dumb luck.

I've experienced a measure of success, especially in my writing life. But if I'm being honest, when I consider the level of success I've had, every significant thing seems to be less about being rewarded for my own efforts and far more about the blessing of God.

Someone might say, "But you had to write really good books to be published so often and win so many writing awards." And I would reply that, even as I write, I receive all kinds of help from God. The best parts of my stories weren't pre-planned and seem to come from beyond my own intellect.

I have concluded, then, that the best place to focus my efforts (whether in writing or in any other facet of life), is to seek out the blessing of God. To pursue those things that God's Word says invite His favor. Things like humility, mercy, faith and obedience. I believe the blessing of God **is the decisive difference in every area of life**.

What is the blessing of God? I like the way Bruce Wilkinson defines God's blessing in his bestselling book, The Prayer of Jabez:

"Notice a radical aspect of Jabez's request for blessing. He left it entirely up to God to decide what the blessings would be and where, when, and how he would receive them. This kind of radical trust in God's good intentions toward us has nothing in common with the popular gospel that you should ask God for a Cadillac, a six-figure income, or some other material sign that you have found a way to cash in on your connection with Him. Instead, the Jabez blessing focuses like a laser on our wanting for ourselves nothing more and nothing less than what God wants for us."

The blessing of God is about being where God has us and learning to be content whether our circumstances are difficult or smooth. And this blessing, I believe, is what makes the decisive difference in the quality of our lives.

Lord, thank You for the greatest blessing...sending Jesus to die in my place, then opening my heart to the gospel. Because of this, I am your child. I want to experience more of Your blessings today. Help me to walk in humility and faith, to show mercy to others. Give me the strength to know and obey Your commands throughout this day, so that I can be a blessing to others also. In Jesus' name, Amen.

Day 13

The Link Between Happiness and Expectations

I used to love roller coasters. The wilder and faster, the better. My wife? Not so much. In fact, my love of roller coasters almost ruined our honeymoon in 1976. We were at Six Flags near Atlanta. After expressing my love for roller coasters, I asked if we could go on the Scream Machine together. It was the wrong question. The right question would have been: "*Do you like roller coasters?*"

But I was nineteen and duller than a five-watt bulb. We went on the Scream Machine. She screamed all right. So did I. The difference was…hers were screams of terror. When the ride ended I asked if she'd like to go on it again. Through tears, she managed to say: "No, thank you. I don't ever want to go on a roller coaster again."

For me, this was a "teaching moment."

Over the years, my wife has relaxed her roller coaster moratorium a little. Certain theme parks have kiddie-coasters that run at slower speeds over smaller hills. No sharp turns and certainly no upside down loops. We've gone on these together. At the end, no screams…happy wife.

I didn't know it then, but this roller coaster experience served as something of a metaphor for the rest of our marriage. On an emotional scale, my life is more like that roller coaster with big ups and downs, crazy speeds and sharp turns. My wife, emotionally speaking, goes through life much more evenly (like that kiddy-coaster).

We've been married thirty-eight years, so we've gone through most of life's trials together. I'm aware by now of a certain pattern, a way we react towards the challenges and disappointments that come our way.

Cindi stays mostly happy. If she gets discouraged at all, she bounces back quickly. Her faith in God is rock solid. Sometimes, I'm all over the place. Like I'm still on the Scream Machine. I get discouraged more often, get hurt more easily, and take longer to recover.

We've talked about why this is so many times (usually when she's trying to help me get to a better place). It has something to do with where we set our expectations. I tend to set mine very high (see the roller coaster car rising, hear the click-click-click sound). But in the real world, almost nothing goes the way I planned. Real life hits and falls so far short of my expectations. When it does, I come crashing down.

Cindi's approach is really rooted in the wisdom of these two Scriptures:

> "*Hope deferred* (i.e. expectations delayed) *makes the heart sick...*" (Prov 13:12)

"*My soul, wait upon God only, for my expectation comes from Him…*" (Psalm 62:5)

She has learned not to set her expectations too high in earthly matters (including people), so when things don't turn out as planned, her emotions don't suffer the consequences. Instead, she looks to God to set her expectations on the things He intends to provide. She knows expectations that come from God will not be disappointed. God has the ability to follow through on every promise He makes.

As a result, in real life, I'm finding it is much more pleasant riding beside her on that kiddy-coaster.

Lord, thank You for being willing to direct not just the big events in my life but also the details. Help me today not to get ahead of You in my thoughts and desires, setting my expectations on everything going a certain way. I don't know the future, but You do. I want Your will to be done, Your kingdom to come. Help me to be more content with letting You be in control of everything today. I know You love me and only want what's best for my life. In Jesus' name, Amen.

Day 14

Praying to a God Who is There

Once during a quiet time, I read a fairly familiar Scripture passage followed by a familiar exhortation. It didn't matter that I had read this passage many times before, or that I had read similar encouraging words before. They still fed my soul and encouraged my heart.

I'm not including the verse here, because our theme today could have happened reading any number of Scripture passages. The verse was about waiting on God and trusting in Him as you wait. It talked about letting God be in control and not giving into fear or anxiety.

I recall thinking it to be rather interesting that such a familiar passage would still speak life to me after four decades of following the Lord pretty closely. You'd think after so much time, the message in this passage would strike me as something of a rerun.

Been there done that.

But it didn't. It was like a drink of fresh, cold water on a blistering day. Like seeing a sign directing you back to the correct road when you've been lost for the last thirty minutes.

I did what the Scripture suggested. I spent time alone

with God, resting in Him, releasing my cares into His control, allowing the Holy Spirit to refresh and strengthen me.

And He did.

He always does whenever I draw near and allow sufficient time for this exchange to take place. Because the God of Abraham, Isaac and Jacob is faithful and His love is everlasting. He is like a living stream that never runs dry. He's been doing this very thing to all those who turn to Him for, literally, thousands of years.

That's why I can read words penned in either the Old or New Testament, by His followers throughout church history, and even by contemporary writers or Christian psalmists writing songs I hear on the radio. All of them telling of this same wonderful exchange that happens whenever God's children turn to Him in times of trouble, instead of turning to other things.

We draw near to Him, and He draws near to us. And then, somehow, His presence brings a peace that surpasses understanding. He calms our fears. He lightens our load. He eases our sorrows. He restores our hope.

This almost universal and timeless experience—this miraculous exchange—can occur for only one reason: Because we are *turning to a God who is There*. Think of the absurdity of sitting all alone in a room, talking to no one but yourself, hoping for relief from an invisible being that doesn't exist and isn't even there.

Nothing would happen. It would be a pathetic waste of time.

Our energies would be better spent drinking a fifth of bourbon, smoking pot or downing some serious narcotics. But these things don't help those who turn to them. They only dull the senses and postpone the suffering. And most of these refuge-idols come with serious, destructive kickbacks.

But we pray to a God who *is* there. A God who *is* paying attention, who *is* willing to help. He will not only work-together-for-good the various circumstances in our lives but He will, in the meantime, offer us the pleasure of His company, which will sustain and strengthen us, as we await His deliverance from all our troubles.

This is not a bad deal. In fact, it's the best of deals. It is welcome news to my soul, no matter how many times I hear it, read it or experience it for myself.

Thank you Lord. I join with all of those who've gone before me to say, there is no one like You, not in Heaven or on the earth. Thank You for being there and for making Your existence and presence known to me. Thank You for giving me your Spirit, who is with me now always. Because He is, I am never alone. Thank you allowing me to draw near you, but even more, for drawing near to me in return. Help me to rest securely in Your love throughout this day. In Jesus' name, Amen.

Day 15
The Hard Work of Believing

*"Then they asked him, "What must we do to do the works God requires?" Jesus answered, "**The work of God is this: to believe** in the one he has sent."* (John 6:28-29, NIV)

After reading this passage during a quiet time, I started thinking about how hard it is to do nothing.

The setting of this passage is simple. Jesus had miraculously fed thousands of people, and now they want to crown Him king. The disciples may have been thrilled at this, but Jesus wasn't. He immediately begins to adjust the crowd's attitude and expectations.

He points out that their real motivation to make Him king is so that He could feed them this way from now on. He tells them the real bread they need is not the bread they typically work for, not even the manna that God gave the Israelites in Moses' time. They need, "the bread that comes down from heaven," speaking figuratively of Himself.

But see how they respond (in the verse above)? They asked Jesus **what work they must do** to receive this blessing from God. When we want something from God, our immediate instinct is often the same, to try and figure out what we must do to get God to act on our behalf. Give us an assignment, we cry; a task, something we can do.

Jesus says to us the same thing He said to them: "*This is the work you need to do…believe in Me.*"

"What?" we reply. "No Lord, you're not getting what I'm saying. I already believe in You. I'm asking for something I can *do* to get You to give me what I'm asking."

The Lord repeats the same thing. And He always will. Because for Him, THIS (that is, believing) is the starting point. For us, it's DOING STUFF.

He wants us to put our trust in Him, first and foremost. To set our entire hope on God being faithful in the matter at hand. He wants us to trust in His wisdom, His timing, even in the methods He chooses to carry out His plan.

This does not come easy to us. We often interpret this as *doing nothing*. But it's actually hard work. At times, very hard. Actively putting our faith and trust in God, and waiting on Him for whatever "work" He wants us to do, requires an enormous amount of effort.

It is the effort of being still. Of quieting our hurried, anxious minds and releasing those tensions to God, rather than acting on them. The Fall has predisposed us to immediately start working to fix whatever is wrong in our lives; to "sew our fig leaves together."

Did you know that every other world religion throughout history and in modern times, except Christianity, includes the idea of man *doing things* to get right with God? The concept of salvation by faith in something God has done for us is a totally foreign concept.

We would never have thought of it.

But Jesus says: "This is the work I'm looking for…believe in Me."

Later, He may very well give us assignments to do, but first He wants us to follow the same pattern He followed with His Father. Jesus focused His attention on watching what the Father was doing and listening for His instructions. Then He acted. That's where God wants us to put our energies, too.

But man…is it hard work.

Lord, You are the Author and Perfecter of our faith. Even the faith we have is a gift from you, not something we have worked up. Still, You call us to exercise our faith and work hard at believing in You and Your faithfulness. Strengthen our hearts to be able to do this more today, to not look at things and try to figure them all out, but to look to You and put our faith in You. In Jesus' name, Amen.

Day 16

Time Gaps

How long is a minute? How many minutes are in an hour? How many hours in a single day? The answer to these questions isn't a matter of opinion. There is only one correct answer to each question. 60 seconds, 60 minutes, 24 hours.

The concept of Time is rooted in fact. It's unambiguous like math. 2 + 2 will ALWAYS = 4.

So why is it, when we're waiting for something we really want to happen, time ticks by so slowly? For me, every minute in a doctor's waiting room feels like five. How about sitting behind a row of cars in the left turn lane at a busy intersection (especially if your car gets stuck waiting through another round when the green arrow turns red again)?

Time crawls by then.

Earlier, I mentioned the biblical concept of "waiting on God." As mentioned in Day 3, doesn't it often feel like God moves much too slowly? Especially when we're crying out for a difficult situation to change?

The Bible is filled with promises that insist God loves us, hears our prayers and has absolute, sovereign power over every aspect of life. Which is why, I think, we struggle when God takes *way* too long to "get it done." If our wait goes on too long, we can begin to doubt the truthfulness of His Word.

I think the real issue stems from our concept of Time. Specifically, how we measure it compared to the language used in Scripture. God chose to write the pages of Scripture two thousand years or more before the age of technology. And He revealed it to generations of people who had a totally different concept of Time.

Life moved at a much slower pace for them, an agricultural pace. Farmers, for example, didn't sow their seed in a field then go out the next day with baskets expecting to fill them with fruit. They didn't stare at the ground uttering profanities because things grew too slow. Crops grew at their *expected pace.*

When they read verses like, "*What a man sows, he will also reap. Sow sparingly, reap sparingly. Sow bountifully, reap bountifully*" (Gal. 6:7; 2 Cor. 9:6) they would instinctively understand **a long time gap** existed between these two events. In reality, it would be "Sow" (*insert lengthy time gap*) then "Reap."

Many Christians today don't get this. We don't allow for time gaps. We set our expectations on modern sensibilities, which is why we're so often frustrated and experience anxiety when unpleasant things keep on happening for much too long.

We want what we want, and we want it now.

We want the situation fixed now. We want the path to

be clear now. We don't want to spend any time living with uncertainty. We want clarity, and answers. *"God, you promised to make the rough places smooth and the crooked ways straight. Well, they still look pretty rough and pretty crooked to me."*

So many promises like that are found in the Bible, and they are still true. But there are time gaps assumed and implied that we, because of our modern concepts of time, fail to see.

Why do these time gaps exist? What is happening during this time when it seems like nothing is happening at all? God is at work, pulling together all the things that need to happen to make everything work together for our good (Rom 8:28).

Are you struggling with any time gap issues today? If so, I suggest you take a few moments and try to recall the times when God's wisdom and faithfulness were proven right, even though it seemed He took way too long at first.

Lord, please forgive me for believing You move too slowly. Or worse, for sometimes believing You aren't doing anything at all. I know that You love me, and that Your ways are rooted in a wisdom that is often too high for me to understand. I release all my pre-set expectations back to You. Help me to become more content with the time gaps You've placed in my life, and to trust that everything going on in my life is still under Your sovereign control. In Jesus' name Amen.

Day 17

Forgetting What God's Already Done

Some time ago, my wife and I were watching a show on our DVR from the History Channel, called *The Bible*. During a segment on Moses, I was freshly inspired about God's ability to liberate Israel after four centuries of slavery. They could not do a thing to free themselves, so He put forth a strategy that involved miraculous feats of supernatural power.

When He was done, they were free.

I thought about what it must have been like for the Jews alive at that time to witness these things, firsthand. You might think a people who saw such extravagant displays of supernatural power would be forever grateful to the One who delivered them. You might think they would also conclude a God who could do all these things could certainly provide for them from now on.

But that's not what we see. Shortly after these events, they begin to grumble and complain at Moses, and at God, with each new trial they face. We're not talking about some minor discouragement here but full-fledged anger and resentment. The shake-your-fist-in-God's-face kind of anger. There was no thankfulness toward God and no willingness to trust Him.

It was as if they had disregarded everything God had done for them so far and adopted this attitude: "*Okay, but what have you done for me lately?*" As I watched these scenes, I found myself criticizing them for being so ungrateful.

Then I began to reflect on some of my own—even fairly recent—episodes of grumbling and complaining. I've been walking with the Lord since the age of seventeen (I'm in my late fifties). I haven't seen God part the Red Sea, but I have witnessed so many miraculous examples of God's love and faithfulness.

And yet, I can still easily adopt a similar: "*Okay, but what have you done for me lately?*" attitude toward God. The truth is, if I would take even a few moments to think about the correct answer to this question, I could come up with a long and growing list of things God *has* done for me. Even lately.

I think this is why the psalmists and even the apostles in the New Testament urge us to cultivate a thankful heart toward God. We need **to regularly and intentionally** dwell on the good things God has done for us. Not because God craves compliments, but because the default setting for our minds is set in the wrong place.

We magnify the negative, the parts left undone, the prayers not yet answered. But what would happen if we deliberately spent time thinking about what God has already done for us? Paul talked about giving thanks all the time, for everything, not just the "big things." And yet, on the whole, his life involved a lot more suffering and hardship than mine.

You'd think Paul would be grumbling and complaining most of the time about how crummy his life was. All he was trying to do was preach the gospel to people. But we don't hear *any* grumbling and complaining from Paul. Instead, he is constantly expressing thanks and telling us to do the same.

Not surprisingly, we also see Paul experiencing a great measure of joy and contentment on a regular basis. Maybe there's a clue here, maybe there's a connection.

So I've started trying to thank God more often. And instead of waiting around for "significant" answers to prayer, I'm thanking Him for ordinary things. And you know what? I'm starting to experience more joy. I'm starting to realize, God has done and is doing all kinds of things in my life that I never noticed before.

How about you? What are some things you are thankful for today? Take a few moments and think about it.

Lord, thank You. Thank You for the big things You have done, like dying on the cross for my sins. For being willing to open my eyes to the gospel. For giving me Your Holy Spirit so that I'm never alone. Help me to start cultivating a more thankful heart, to not only see these things, but all the little evidences of Your love and kindness that I take for granted most of the time. I know they are there. Help me to see them more often. In Jesus' name, Amen.

Day 18

Accentuate the Positive

Remember this golden oldie tune? *"You've got to…accentuate the positive and…eliminate the negative…"* The song goes on urging us to latch onto the affirmative, and not to mess with *"Mr. In-Between."* When I occasionally hear that song, it sticks in my head for days. It was recorded *way* back in 1944, during WWII. It's a catchy, fun song, but it also offers some sound biblical advice.

CS Lewis indirectly talked about this theme in a sermon called *The Weight of Glory*; about the tendency to spend so much energy suppressing negative and unhealthy desires, when the desires for the things of God are so much more fulfilling:

"It would seem that Our Lord finds our desires not too strong, but too weak. We are half-hearted creatures, fooling about with drink and sex and ambition when infinite joy is offered us, like an ignorant child who wants to go on making mud pies in a slum because he cannot imagine what is meant by the offer of a holiday at the sea. We are far too easily pleased."

— CS Lewis

I think Christians often get confused on this point and, because we do, we often wear ourselves out resisting sinful desires, rather than re-directing our energy toward all the great things God has given us to do.

For example, the Bible doesn't tell us just to focus on being "dead to sin," but also to be "alive to God" (Rom. 6:11). We're not just told to "put off the old self," but "put on the new" (Eph. 4:24). Not just to "resist the devil" but also to "humble yourself before God" (Jam. 4:7). In other words, we're not to use all our energy constantly suppressing the negative but, instead, *redirecting that energy* into opening our hearts completely to God and giving Him all we've got.

When we do this, our tank doesn't become empty because God keeps filling it back up again with more of Him. That's why our load stays light (Matt. 11:30). When we're abiding in Jesus, He carries the greater weight, so we don't get weary as we serve. The assumption is always that we're serving from the strength we've received.

I think this is why we constantly hear the apostle Paul talking about this abounding joy he's experiencing in his walk with the Lord. Even though he was constantly pouring out his life serving others and suffering on a regular basis. Not exactly activities we typically associate with abundant joy.

But this joy was real for Paul. Despite his challenges, being joyful was the *norm* for Paul. I believe that's God's intention for us, too, as an outflow of living by grace. And when we do, it changes everything.

Properly understood, receiving grace results in MORE doing, not inactivity or sloppy living. Paul was a champion of God's grace and yet, really, did anyone work harder than Paul? Was anyone more zealous to obey and please God than him? The difference in our fruitfulness is amazing when we set our focus on receiving life from the vine rather than on what's happening at the end of our branches.

How about you? If we hooked you up to a "Joy Meter" where would the needle go? Are you experiencing a yoke that is easy and a burden that feels light? (Matt. 11:28-30).

Lord Jesus, thank You for Your amazing grace. You have set things up so that we can always draw near to Your throne of grace and receive all the help we need, no matter what we're going through. We're grateful that You don't resent our weakness, but welcome us just the way we are. Help us to remain aware of Your Presence throughout this day, and to catch those negative thoughts and the enemy's lies, before they take root. In Jesus' name, Amen.

Day 19

The Value of Hard Times

I've attended many small gatherings of Christians over the years. Often such meetings end with the leader asking if there are any prayer requests. People then share specific things they want group members to pray for. On the way home from one of these meetings, it dawned on me that almost every prayer request involved people asking for troubling things in their life to stop, for problems to go away or be solved, and various aspects of their life to be dramatically improved.

In short, everyone was asking God to bring their trials and troubling circumstances to a quick end. Isn't this the content of most people's prayers? A little self-examination quickly resulted in me adding myself to this fairly large group.

These observations brought me to this conclusion: **Being a faithful Christian doesn't bring an end to the troubles and difficulties of life**. They continue to happen throughout our lives, like they do for people who don't follow the Lord or even attempt to obey God's commands.

In light of this, why would we imagine we can pray our troubles away? Where does this expectation come from?

Scripture would seem to encourage the *opposite* view:

- *"In the world you **will have** tribulation..."* (John 16:33, ESV, Jesus speaking)
- *"Count it all joy **when** you fall into various trials..."* (James 1:2, NKJV)
- *"For when we came into Macedonia, we had no rest, but we were troubled **at every turn**—conflicts on the outside, fears within."* (2 Cor. 7:5, NIV, Paul speaking)

These are just a few of the dozen or more Scriptures that come to mind. Can you think of any promises of trouble-free living in the Bible? No?

If this is true (that we shouldn't expect a trouble-free life), is there **any benefit to becoming a Christian at all, at least in this life?** I add that phrase at the end, because faith in Christ certainly makes all the difference in the life to come (i.e. Heaven).

I believe the answer is a definite and emphatic YES! I can think of at least 4 distinct benefits in following Christ, even in the midst of ongoing trials:

1. Obeying Christ and following His commands eliminates an entire layer of "extra" troubles that come as very-real consequences of a disobedient life. Non-Christians (and disobedient Christians) experience far more trials in this life, as they heap

upon themselves additional troubles through misguided and selfish choices.

2. The Lord promises to draw near to us in our troubles, if we turn to Him in prayer. He promises to give us a peace that surpasses understanding and a joy that comes from being in His presence (even if the trial continues).

3. He promises to work everything in our lives (even our trials) together for our good, so that our trials are not pointless. Our troubles are actually leading to a conclusion personally supervised by God.

4. God promises to use our trials the way fire refines and purifies gold, to form within us more fully the character and nature of His Son (the fruit of the Spirit), as we respond to them in faith, trust and obedience.

These are not small or insignificant things but serious reasons to rejoice and be glad even when things don't go our way. Can you think of other benefits of following Christ in this life, besides the four I've cited?

Lord, thank You for the big difference You make during my trials. Forgive me for grumbling and complaining, and for clinging to a wrong expectation that in this world my life should be trouble-free. That's not what Your Word says. Help me to cultivate a healthier outlook that is mostly aware of the benefits I receive because You are with me and for me, even in the most challenging of times. In Jesus' name, Amen.

Day 20

Thankfulness and Joy

Thankfulness is a theme we need to spend a little more time on, because the gravitational pull of this world continually draws us away from this.

If a car was parked on a flat surface and set in neutral gear, nothing would happen. It would likely remain at the same place. But what if the car was parked on a hill and you put it in neutral? What would happen? It would begin to slide downward.

That's what we're dealing with, spiritually speaking. We don't live on level ground. Adam's Fall has placed all of us on an upward slant, on a hill. As a result, if we become spiritually lazy or passive, like that car set in neutral gear, we can easily slide downward into grumbling at God or becoming irritable and annoyed with others.

It's not something we have to work at. It's where our hearts naturally go without effort. Thankfully this force is not insurmountable; the hill is not all that steep. But to offset this tendency to slide downward, we have to do something deliberate, to exert a measure of effort.

Continuing our metaphor a little more, we must put our car in gear and step on the gas. The gas pedal for the

Christian is thanksgiving, or thankfulness. I'm not exactly sure how it works (I don't get how car engines work, either) but it most definitely does.

Somehow, the grace of God works through thankfulness to create joy in our hearts. I can be bored—or worse, grumbling and discouraged. If I simply shift my heart a little, and begin thanking the Lord for things, my mind is soon brimming over with fresh reasons to be thankful. I become much more aware of the goodness of God in my life, and see all these good things He has done.

It's like going from Zero to Joy in sixty seconds.

I'm not talking about making up things to thank God for that aren't really there. I'm simply doing what David explains in Psalm 40:

"Oh Lord my God, you have performed many wonders for us. Your plans for us are too numerous to list. You have no equal. IF I TRIED to recite all your wonderful deeds, I would never come to the end of them." (Ps. 40:5).

David found that the issue is not a shortage of activity on God's part. It's a question of where *our* minds are focused. IF we'd set them on thankfulness, we would find abundant evidence of God's love, goodness and faithfulness in our lives.

IF we would.

And IF we would, we would very quickly experience the same result David talks about a few verses later: "*I take joy in doing your will, my God, for your instructions are written in my heart.*"

I think joy is preferable to grumbling and

discouragement, don't you? I believe there is a direct correlation between thankfulness and contentment. There's an old saying: "*Contentment comes not from getting what you want, but wanting what you have.*"

I would add, the trick of wanting what we have is taking stock of where we've set our focus. Is it on all the things we don't like or don't have right now, or on all the things we do have but are no longer thankful for?

Spend some time thinking and thanking God for the things He's already done. When you do, you'll see the list grow right before your eyes. And as you thank Him, watch how quickly joy begins to grow in your heart.

Lord, I realize now that I've been far too passive in my outlook. I haven't been living aware of the fact that my life in this world is lived "on a hill," not on level ground. Far too often, I slide easily into grumbling and complaining. Help me to reset my focus today on who You are and what You've already done in my life. Help me to cultivate a thankful heart, so I can experience a greater measure of joy. Help me begin to see all the examples of Your love all around me. In Jesus' name, Amen.

Day 21
Setting Our Minds

As I mentioned near the beginning of this book, Jesus placed a great deal of value on the Holy Spirit as the One who makes all the difference in a believer's life (remember what He said during the Last Supper?). The apostle Paul also placed the same high value on the Holy Spirit in his life and urges us to do the same.

"*For those who live according to the flesh set their minds on the things of the flesh, but those who live according to the Spirit **set their minds on the things of the Spirit**. To set the mind on the flesh is death, but **to set the mind on the Spirit is life and peace**.*" (Rom. 8:5-6, ESV)

In this passage, Paul talks about the importance of "*setting our minds on the Spirit.*" Did you know that our minds needed to be deliberately set on the Holy Spirit? It's been my experience that failing to do this results in my mind setting itself on "the other dial."

I believe this passage also highlights an important reason believers should establish a quiet time every morning. It's a perfect time to set our minds on the right dial; that is, on the Holy Spirit.

It has become my habit to do this, awaking each day

then, fairly early on, surrendering my heart and mind to the Holy Spirit's control. It's made a vital difference in the quality of my life.

When I don't live with my mind set on the Spirit, I am almost a totally different person. Here are some of the things I've observed. They're not good things. My mind is almost always thinking. I can become easily annoyed. I tend to worry about many things. I can become preoccupied. When that happens, I'm not a good listener. I have less compassion for the lost.

As time goes on, I can become critical and fault-finding, self-absorbed, sometimes craving the recognition and the approval of others. I rarely encourage others and, perhaps worst of all…I don't even realize I am acting this way.

Oh, and I have almost no joy or peace.

See what I mean? See why it matters?

When Paul said "to set the mind on the flesh is death," I don't believe he was referring to physical death, but a very real death just the same. A total absence of life and peace. The difference is that dramatic.

When I walk humbly dependent on the Holy Spirit, I am none of the things and do none of the things I listed above. My mind is mostly still and at rest. I care deeply about others. I meditate often on the Word. I think of and thank God often for what He's done and is doing in me. I have real joy and even seem joyful to others. I feel compassion for others. I pray easily and desire to pray throughout the day.

I could go on...but you get the idea.

Life or death, this is the difference between a mind set on the Spirit or on the flesh.

Paul realized this truth and realized the tremendous difference it makes when we deliberately and intentionally set our minds on the Spirit every day. You can do this right now, and every other morning. It's a choice God invites us to make every day.

Lord, thank You for giving Your Holy Spirit to me, so that at all times, no matter where I go, I'm always connected with You. But now I see the need to be more intentional about setting my mind on Your Spirit. I want to do that right now. I recognize the pitfalls of a life set on the flesh. I've experienced this, and I don't want to walk like that anymore. I want to experience Your presence more fully in my life today, and from now on. In Jesus' name, Amen.

Day 22
How Often God Thinks About Us

"Many, O Lord My God, are the wonders You have done, and Your thoughts toward us; there is none to compare with You. If I would declare and speak of them they would be too numerous to count." (Psalm 40:5, NASB)

I believe the entire Bible is the inspired Word of God. I don't believe some verses are true and others are not. Or, that I can choose to believe certain verses I like and ignore other verses I don't like as much. Having said that, sometimes when I read the Bible in my quiet time, some verses do seem to *impact me* more on a personal level than others.

This happened one morning while reading the verse above. Before reading, I had been thanking God for delivering me from a serious trial we had been going through for several months. I liked what I read in the first four verses of the psalm but, when I read the fifth verse, it was as if I had been walking up a hill for a while and suddenly found myself staring at a magnificent view. The reality behind these words stunned me. They are so magnificent, I find them almost hard to believe.

David starts off acknowledging the many wonders God has done. This concept is not hard for me to grasp. Just spending a little time observing and dwelling on the beauty of God's creation has that effect on me. A gorgeous sunset. A full moon coming up over the ocean. A crisp, starry night. A drive through the mountains. Occasionally, I'll come across a collection of mind-blowing photographs on the internet, all illustrating the wonders God has accomplished on earth and in the heavens.

I agree with David. *"Many, O Lord My God, are the wonders You have done…"* It's the **next** thing David said that jumped off the page for me: *"…and Your thoughts toward us…If I would declare and speak of them they would be too numerous to count."*

How is it possible that Almighty God—the Creator of all things, ruler of the Universe, the Lord of History—has more thoughts toward me than can be counted? David is saying that God doesn't just think about me every now and then, which by itself would be amazing. He is saying that God has so many thoughts about me they are too numerous to count.

As I thought about this, I remembered something that Jesus said in the gospels: *"What is the price of two sparrows—one copper coin? But not a single sparrow can fall to the ground without your Father knowing it. And the very hairs on your head are all numbered."* (Matt. 10:29-30)

It's hard for our finite minds to get a handle on someone possessing this capacity for knowledge. Like most men, I cannot multi-task. Simply put, I can't even juggle two things at a time. If I'm watching a TV show, and you ask me to read something, the TV show ceases to exist as I read.

God is not like that, which is a major understatement. He has an *infinite* capacity to multi-task. Jesus isn't saying this to brag or boast about His Father's intellect. He's saying that if God has the capacity to know when a single sparrow falls to the ground, and can even tell us the exact number of hairs on our head at any given moment, He can certainly look after us and supervise our affairs on a personal level.

We have no reason to fear. God is not just All-Powerful, He is All-Knowing and All-Caring. He knows us better and knows more about us than the closest friend we've ever had. Better than we even know ourselves.

Who am I, O Lord, that You should even consider me, let alone think about me so often? I praise You for the way, no...for the many ways, You demonstrate Your love and care for me. I may be just a number or a meaningless cog in the wheel to others, but not to You. You are intimately acquainted with all my ways. Help me to rest today in the sure knowledge that You are paying attention to everything going on in my life, and that You have it all under Your control. In Jesus' name, Amen.

Day 23

God is Not Discouraged By Our Weakness

Occasionally, I get discouraged.

Especially when I fail God in some way. I hate it when my responses and reactions to situations fall short of what I know they should be. But the truth is, sometimes I'm weak.

Knowing the right way to be or the right thing to do doesn't mean I'll always do it. Thankfully, if I do stumble and fall then turn to God and ask His forgiveness, God *is faithful and just to forgive us our sins and cleanse us from all unrighteousness* (1 John 1:9).

Even so, it can be discouraging when we have to turn to God for mercy once again, because we've stumbled in some way. Once during a bout with this kind of discouragement, the Spirit began to "breathe courage into me" (the definition of encouragement) by bringing certain Scriptures to my mind:

> "*Now may the God of peace…equip you with everything good that you may do His will, **working in us** that which is pleasing in His sight, through Jesus Christ…*" (Heb. 13:20-21, ESV)

71

*"And I am sure of this, that He who began **a good work in you**, will bring it to completion at the day of Jesus Christ."* (Phil. 1:6, ESV)

*"For it is God who **works within you**, both to will and to do of His good pleasure."* (Phil. 2:13, NKJV)

Each of these verses speak of the fact that God lives within me now and is working within me to help me accomplish the things that please Him. I am not down here all by myself trying to make a go of it, hoping I succeed. It also dawned on me that if God lives within me, then He is not surprised nor discouraged by my weaknesses or failures.

I'm not saying they don't matter, or that I shouldn't take them seriously. But discouragement is never a fruitful place to live. Discouragement paralyses; it gives up hope; it moves our hearts away from faith toward unbelief. It whispers in our ear: *"Why even try anymore?"*

Well, here's why. If God hasn't given up on me, why should I give up on Him, or on the work He is accomplishing within me? God does not get discouraged when I fail, because He has supreme confidence in the power of the Holy Spirit to, *"work in me that which is pleasing in His sight."* He doesn't see me as I am right now, but as I will be when the transforming power of His Spirit wins the day. He sees my weakness giving way to His strength. When it does, it will not be some earthly, counterfeit strength, but a strength that comes directly from Him.

Consider for a moment the confidence Christ had going forward to the cross when, just the night before at the Last Supper, it was apparent His disciples still "didn't get it." What they "didn't get" were some of the major themes Jesus had taught them over the past three years. But we don't see any fear in Jesus for their future. He had supreme confidence in the power of the Spirit to "*work in them that which is pleasing in His sight.*"

That's the same promise He makes to us.

Meditating on this encourages me and fills me with hope. Not in myself but in the work the Holy Spirit will accomplish, and the changes that work will make in me as I begin to depend more and more on His strength instead of mine.

Lord, thank You for the permanent commitment and investment You have made in my life. Thank You for the gift of Your Holy Spirit, and for the promises You have made to continue to work within me, no matter what. Because of this, I can look to the future with hope and not stay paralyzed by discouragement. Help me become more aware of Your presence in my life today, and to cooperate more fully with Your plans for me today. In Jesus' name, Amen.

Day 24

Tolerating Low-Grade Anxiety

"Anxiety is like a mild case of atheism."

I'm not sure who said this first, but the first time I heard it, I instantly connected with its meaning. I think it's fair to say that being a Christian and being an atheist are mutually exclusive (you can't be both things at the same time). A Christian comes down solidly on the "Yes" side of the question: *Does God really exist?"*

An atheist says No.

But just how solid is our Yes to the existence of God? And what kind of God do we really believe in? Is God all-powerful? Is He all-loving? Is He both at the same time? The Bible teaches that He is.

So...if God is all-powerful then there's nothing He cannot do to help me. None of the things beyond my control are beyond His. However, being all-powerful doesn't necessarily mean God *will* help me, or that He will take care of everything beyond my control.

For that to happen, He must be all-loving also. On that point, the Bible boldly declares, "God is love" (1 John 4:8). Then I should be fine, right? His love ensures that He will use his almighty power to take care of me and direct the affairs of my life in a benevolent, loving way.

If all these things are true, then why would I ever worry?

Exactly.

During a recent season of uncertainty, the Holy Spirit showed me a kind of anxiety I still casually tolerate in my heart and mind. It's a special brand of anxiety that runs beneath the surface, like a low-grade fever. Often beyond my detection.

It occurs whenever I am worrying about **someone or something I am responsible for**. At such times, I can get so deeply concerned that it's almost painful. The whole time, I don't usually view it as anxiety. I am just...*concerned*. I'm just caring about something (or someone) that I am supposed to care about this intently.

If I don't, who will? (Are you starting to see where this is going?). The implication is...*not God*.

But now I see this kind of care is not really what it seems. This "low-grade anxiety" does nothing more than rob me of joy and peace. Not all at once and not in a way that's even obvious to those around me. At least, not at first.

Left to itself, over time this fever can grow, especially if I don't see it for what it truly is. It's not being responsible. It's just anxiety. I am not trusting God.

Something very well may be happening to someone or something I am responsible for, but I have forgotten (at least temporarily) that I am not on my own here. There is a God in Heaven. A God who is both all-powerful AND all-loving. And He doesn't hold me responsible for things beyond my control. He's even willing to help with things I have some measure of control over.

One of the last things Jesus said to His apostles before His ascension was, "*I will be with you always, even to the end of the age*" (Matt. 28:20). During the Last Supper, again, speaking of the Holy Spirit, Jesus said: "*...He will be with you forever*" (John 14:16). In his letter to the Philippians, Paul wrote, "*Be anxious for nothing*" (Phil. 4:6).

I looked it up. In the Greek, **nothing means nothing**. That includes any and every situation we are worrying about (even a situation we are responsible for).

Lord, forgive me for temporarily forgetting that You do exist, and that You do care about everything going on in my life, including this current situation. You are faithful. I don't need to worry that You will fail to do Your part. I surrender complete control of it, and my entire life, back into Your capable hands. Thank You for Your mercy and kindness, that they are new every morning. And that Your ability to do all things remains completely intact. In Jesus' name, Amen.

Day 25

God Gives Us the Lighter Load to Carry

During one particular quiet time, I was feeling a little confused and began to ask God to show me what was going on in my heart and mind, similar to the way David prayed in Psalm 139:23-24:

> *"Search me, God, and know my heart; test me and know my anxious thoughts. See if there is any offensive way in me, and lead me in the way everlasting."*

I had been facing another time of uncertainty and wrestling with anxiety. I wanted to break free of it and trust God completely throughout the day. More than that, I wanted to be able to trust Him until the situation had resolved to the place it needed to be.

The Holy Spirit directed me to three Bible passages that worked together to clarify where I was and where I needed to be.

> *"Trust in the Lord with all your heart and do not lean on your own understanding. In all your ways acknowledge Him, and He will make your paths*

straight. Do not be wise in your own eyes; fear the Lord and turn away from evil. It will be healing to your body and refreshment to your bones." (Prov. 3:5-8, NASB)

"Come to Me, all who are weary and heavy-laden, and I will give you rest. Take My yoke upon you and learn from Me, for I am gentle and humble in heart, and you will find rest for your souls. For My yoke is easy and My burden is light." (Matt. 11:28-30, NASB)

"Now we who have believed enter that rest... There remains, then, a Sabbath-rest for the people of God; for anyone who enters God's rest also rests from their works, just as God did from his. Let us, therefore, make every effort to enter that rest, so that no one will perish by following their example of disobedience." (Heb. 4:3, 9-11, NIV)

The basic problem was pretty clear after that. I was not trusting God for the situation. A part of me wanted to, but I was afraid that if I let go of this burden and trusted the Lord completely, He might not fix it, or else He would respond too slowly and the situation would go on a whole lot longer (much longer than if I remained in charge).

The next problem was that my level of weariness and pressure greatly increased because the load I was carrying was too much for me. I couldn't fix it. The real solutions were entirely out of my reach. Another factor was the fear that, if I let go and stopped being in charge, I might miss the cue from God when it came time for me to do something. And the situation would get worse because of my neglect.

I now could see all of this was rooted in unbelief. This is why I was unable to enter into the rest God was willing to give me.

Trusting in the Lord with all our hearts does not mean we have no part to play. Jesus said to take His yoke and carry the burden He gives. The difference is, **God gives us a lighter load to carry than the one we've been carrying**. A load that will not overwhelm us or weigh us down. He takes the heavy load, because He is the only one who can. When we enter into His rest, we release Him to do His sovereign work, as well as to show us the smaller role we are to play.

Whenever we find ourselves getting weary, feeling weighed down, or having little joy or peace inside, we need to recognize these are indicators that we have lost our way. We've picked up a load we were never meant to carry.

Jesus, I confess I have become weary and burdened by this situation. I cannot carry it any longer. I release it entirely into Your hands, Your capable hands. I know Your will likely will involve me in some way, but I need Your help to recognize the lighter load I am supposed to carry. Thank You that Your load is easy and Your burden is light, and that You are willing to do all the heavy lifting in my life. Help me to enter into Your rest of for the rest of this day. In Jesus' name, Amen.

Day 26

Trusting in the Bigness of God

"The heavens declare the glory of God; the skies proclaim the work of his hands. Day after day they pour forth speech; night after night they reveal knowledge." (Psalm 19:1-2, NIV)

One of the great benefits of daily drawing near to God and seeking Him in every situation, even with small challenges, is that it becomes much easier to trust Him when big trials come. I'm finding that, in them, God is bigger still. Of course, God isn't growing. My awareness of His presence and His power is growing. This awareness helps me to experience His Perfect Peace more consistently.

If you're having difficulty getting a breakthrough when your trials seem a bit overwhelming, may I suggest following David's advice in the passage above?

I live near the beach in Florida. No matter how stressed out I may get about the uncertain events in my life, taking a long, slow walk on a mostly-uninhabited stretch of beach does wonders for my soul. I'm not exactly sure why. There's just something about the bigness of the sky at the beach, especially during a sunrise. It has the same effect watching a full moon slide up from below the horizon at night.

Maybe it's the steady lapping of the waves, or the vastness of the ocean itself, stretching out as far as the eye can see. It goes down deeper than the highest mountains in the Himalayas. And yet, the whole of it remains safely at the edge of predetermined boundaries, governed by tides that move slowly in and out twice a day. They do this at intervals so precise we can mark down the time, to the minute, on a little board by the lifeguard station.

Who really controls these things? Who created them as they are by the power of His spoken Word? It is the God to whom we pray.

Our God is a very big God.

Being in the mountains has the same effect on me as walking on the beach. However big my problems may seem at the time, they are instantly shrunk to their proper size when set against the backdrop of the Rockies or the Great Smoky Mountains.

How can a God responsible for creating such majesty in nature have any difficulty sorting out and solving the troubles of a single human being?

If you can't get to the beach or to the mountains, take a walk outside at night. Or drive someplace outside the city lights. Get out of the car, set a lounge chair or blanket down on the ground and just look up. Take in the vastness and the beauty of the moon and the stars. As David says, listen as "*they pour forth speech*" and "*reveal knowledge.*"

Their message is clear: The God who made them has

made you also. This same God loves you and is willing to personally direct and supervise your affairs. He has even promised to work together for good every circumstance in your life, including your present troubles (Rom. 8:28).

In another Psalm, David contrasts these two themes: The bigness of God directing his gaze toward us. *"When I look at the night sky and see the work of your fingers—the moon and the stars you set in place—what are mere mortals that you should think about them, human beings that you should care for them?"* (Psalm 8:3-4, NLT).

When David—a man like us, who often faced serious, even life-threatening trials—considered these things, he declared: *"Oh Lord, our Lord, how majestic is Your Name!"*

Lord Jesus, we agree with David that Your name is indeed majestic. Your power and Your glory are displayed throughout the earth, and far above the earth in the wonders of the universe You have made. Help me to grasp it, that You are the same Being who made both me and all of these things. And that, because You are, I have nothing to fear. You are well able and, more importantly, very willing to help me in this situation. I release it again into your capable hands. In Jesus' name, Amen.

Day 27

More On Living One Day at a Time

Back on Day 10, we talked about the need to center our lives on the day at hand. To learn how to live one day at a time, actively resisting the urge to focus on the things we might face tomorrow, next week, next month, or beyond.

Now, as we're nearing the end of the month, I thought we should re-visit this theme once more. I can think of at least four reasons to do this:

- Reason #1 – There's absolutely no encouragement to live this way in our modern culture. Almost every influence pushes us to live the exact opposite of this approach. Everything is high-tech and fast-paced. Not only should we move fast, we need to think everything through and plan ahead.

- Reason #2 - This is how Jesus lived (one day at a time) and how He tells us to live.

  (Jesus speaking) *Pray then like this: "Our Father in heaven, hallowed be your name. Your kingdom come, your will be done, on earth as it* *is in heaven. **Give us this day** our daily bread…"* (Matt. 6:9-11, ESV)

"So don't worry about tomorrow, for tomorrow will bring its own worries. Today's trouble is enough for today." (Matt. 6:34, NLT)

Then he said to the crowd, *"If any of you wants to be my follower, you must turn from your selfish ways, **take up your cross daily**, and follow me."* (Luke 9:23, NLT)

- <u>Reason #3</u> – God gives us grace for today, not "grace in advance." That's why when we start trying to figure out and solve all the "what-ifs" and "maybes" of tomorrow, we become anxious and worried and soon lose any sense of joy and peace.

- <u>Reason #4</u> – If you think about it, did any of our past situations ever happen the way we planned or imagined? No, they didn't. Every week things happen that we did not expect and could not anticipate. Problems surprise us. Even God's blessings surprise us. Which is why it makes no sense to plan or worry over tomorrow's troubles. Any such plans will turn out to be just as futile…every time.

Some time ago, I read a book, *Experiencing God*, by

evangelical pastor and author Henry Blackaby (*Broadman & Holman Publishers, 1994*). He has a lot of great things to say about the importance of living for the Lord one day at a time. Here are some of my favorite quotes from that book:

> "If you were to do everything that Jesus tells you to do **one day at a time**, you would always be right in the center of where God wants you to be. Can you trust God to guide you that way?"

> "You might think that Jesus would rather you wait until He tells you all the details before you start to follow Him. But that is not the pattern we see in His life or in the Scriptures…He is more likely to call you to follow **one day at a time** than He is to spell out all the details before you begin to obey Him."

> "I have found in my own life that I can release the way (the plan) to Him. Then I take care of everything He tells me **one day at a time**. He gives me plenty to do to fill each day with meaning and purpose."

Lord, thank You for being in charge of my life. I put my trust in You to lead and guide me through this day. Help me to rest in Your plan and Your wisdom, especially when things happen I do not understand. Give me the strength to focus only on the things You are asking of me today, and to resist worrying about tomorrow, or the days after that. In Jesus' name, Amen.

Day 28

Learning to Appreciate Solitude

When I was younger, the world was a much quieter place. It could be noisy on occasion, but finding moments of solitude weren't hard to come by. Take smart phones for starters, and the internet.

They didn't exist.

Typically, there were blocks of time every day when people could not get hold of you, even for something important (let alone something as trivial as a new selfie they just posted on Instagram or Facebook). There weren't any voicemails, or even phone-message machines. You wouldn't know if someone had even tried to call.

If you had a thought to call someone, you couldn't do it, unless you were at home sitting by a telephone. We had phone booths, but they were such a hassle; nobody used them unless you absolutely had to.

If you went out for a walk or a run, you didn't have the option of plugging in your headphones or ear buds to listen to music or a podcast. It was just you, walking or running alone.

There weren't any Tweets, texts, or emails. You couldn't send them and no one ever sent them to you. If you were curious about something, you couldn't Google it. You just thought about it for a while, then gave up, usually never finding out the answer.

All these moments now when our days are interrupted by technology and social media...they didn't happen then. They were quiet moments. Often moments alone.

Life during Bible times contained even more moments of quiet and solitude than my childhood years. They didn't have things like TV, movies and radio back then. No cars, motorcycles or trucks driving on paved roads or highways.

If you wanted to go someplace, usually you walked. For miles. And it would take hours. Most of the time you walked in silence. Except for the occasional sounds of nature. The wind blowing, a bird chirping, the buzzing of an insect. Lots and lots of time for quiet and solitude.

Why does this matter? When the Bible speaks of cultivating a strong devotional relationship with God, the best atmosphere is usually quiet and solitude.

> *"Be still before the Lord and wait patiently for him..."* (Psalms 37:7)

> *"Be still, and know that I am God..."* (Psalms 46:10)

> *"For God alone, O my soul, wait in silence, for my hope is from him."* (Psalms 62:5, ESV)

> *For thus said the Lord God, the Holy One of Israel,*

"In repentance and rest you shall be saved; in quietness and in confidence shall be your strength." (Isaiah 30:15, NKJV)

Even Jesus spent significant times alone. Mark 1:35 says, *"And rising very early in the morning, while it was still dark, He departed and went out to a desolate place, and there He prayed."* There are many more examples like this in the gospels (which we'll see in Day 31).

In Matt. 6:6, after His disciples asked Jesus to teach them how to pray, He said, *"But when you pray, go into your room and shut the door and pray to your Father who is in secret, and your Father who sees in secret will reward you."*

If we ever hope to experience a quiet time today, we must make it happen ourselves. We must carve out blocks of time to meet with God in secret. A quiet time and a quiet place, that's what we need. A place of solitude, where we can meet with God, and He can meet with us.

Lord Jesus, I want to meet with You this way. I want to become more comfortable in quiet times and solitude. Help me to pull away from the hectic and hurried pace of life and learn how to be still. Thank You for being so willing to draw near to me, whenever I do. Even now, I ask You to fill me with Your peace and Your strength, to face whatever I will encounter as this day unfolds. In Jesus' name, Amen.

Day 29

Waiting, Trusting and Following

The entries in this 31-Day Devotional originally came from my personal journal. A journal I began back in 2006 after God led me through something of a personal revival. By that time, I had been a pastor for about twenty-one years.

To understand what I'm about to say, we need to understand the New Testament story of two sisters, named Martha and Mary.

As Jesus and his disciples were on their way, he came to a village where a woman named Martha opened her home to him. She had a sister called Mary, who sat at the Lord's feet listening to what he said. But Martha was distracted by all the preparations that had to be made. She came to him and asked, "Lord, don't you care that my sister has left me to do the work by myself? Tell her to help me!"

"Martha, Martha," the Lord answered, "You are worried and upset about many things, but few things are needed—or indeed only one. Mary has chosen what is better, and it will not be taken away from her." (Luke 10:38-42, NIV)

In the years before becoming a pastor and for several years after, you could say I was more like Mary. I had cultivated a healthy devotional life with God and almost always sought to spend time with Him alone at the beginning of each day. As the busy years of pastoring a growing church took hold, somewhere along the way I became more of a Martha: "...*distracted by all the preparations that had to be made.*"

Being very busy serving God had taken priority over spending adequate time "*sitting at the Lord's feet listening to what he said.*"

During those Martha years, God was patient and kind to me, but He finally got my undivided attention in 2006. I saw how far off the mark I had drifted. The three words that best summarize my life before that were: **Worrying, Striving and Controlling**. Of course, I didn't see this at the time, but it was still the truth. In 2006, I repented and began asking God to help me become a "Mary" once again.

He did.

Since then, I have continued to pursue living a life of dependence on Him, day by day, instead of relying on myself. I thought about the three words that might better sum up the direction I am going now, and came up with: **Waiting, Trusting and Following**.

Here are three of my favorite verses on each of these far-better life themes:

*"**Wait** patiently for the Lord. Be brave and courageous. Yes, wait patiently for the Lord."* (Psalm 27:14, NLT)

*"**Trust** in the Lord with all your heart; and lean not unto your own understanding. In all your ways acknowledge him, and he shall direct your paths."* (Prov. 3:5-6, NKJV)

*"If any man serves me, let him **follow** me; and where I am, there shall also my servant be: if any man serves me, him will my Father honor."* (John 12:26, NKJV)

Living this way, more like Mary, is far better, in every respect. I may not be in control anymore but, it turns out, I never was. Now I live with the certainty that He holds my hand. And since God knows what He's doing and where I am going…what is there to fear?

So, I will **wait** upon Him in whom my soul **trusts** and **follow** where He leads.

Lord, thank You for all the times You've been patient with me when I've been too busy to notice that serving You isn't nearly as important as being with You. Thank You for restoring my heart and renewing my mind, more and more each day, as I sit and listen to what You have to say. Your Words and Your presence have changed my life forever. Give me the strength, this day, to once again wait, trust and follow. In Jesus' name, Amen.

Day 30

A Much Better Peace

"Don't worry about anything; instead, pray about everything. Tell God what you need, and thank him for all he has done. **Then you will experience God's peace, which exceeds anything we can understand.** *His peace will guard your hearts and minds as you live in Christ Jesus."* (Phil. 4:6-7, NLT)

In my journey to experience God's peace in a more consistent way, this passage has become a favorite. Some translations begin with, *"Be anxious for nothing..."* Worry, anxiety, fear, fretting and the more common term used today "stressed out," are all talking about the same thing.

Whatever term we use, Paul is telling us not to give in to it at any time. Be anxious for *nothing.* Don't worry about *anything.* These are absolute terms, which means there's never a time when we should tolerate the presence of worry or anxiety in our lives.

Easier said than done, right? Not really.

Paul doesn't just tell us to stop worrying, he explains what we should do instead. How to redirect the energy we've been wasting on worry. Instead of worrying, which has absolutely no value and won't improve our situation one bit (Matt. 6:7), Paul says we should pray. Talk to God about everything we are thinking (and worrying about). Ask for His help. Make the requests specific.

Paul adds in the phrase: "...*and thank Him for all He's done.*" How does it make sense to be thankful for something we've just prayed about? God hasn't done anything yet. The prayer hasn't been answered yet. The point of expressing thanks (at the same time we are praying about things that bother us) is to re-set our focus on the goodness of God.

Thankfulness redirects our mind, which previously may have been obsessing over something we can't control, while virtually ignoring the multitude of good things God has already done for us. It helps to put the problem we've been worrying about in perspective. A perspective that properly includes a God who cares deeply about us and has the power to deliver us from every difficulty and hardship.

Paul then explains what will happen next, if we follow his advice. A divine transaction will occur. As we wait quietly in His presence, the anxiety that had just moments ago been plaguing us and bringing us down, will be replaced by a gift from God: "*Then you will experience God's peace, **which exceeds anything we can understand.**"*

Another translation calls this, "a peace that *surpasses* understanding." Isn't that what we crave when we are worrying about something? To understand what is going on and how it will be resolved? And when it will be resolved?

Paul is admitting there is a peace that comes from understanding our situation. But he's telling us, the peace that God gives *surpasses* the peace that comes from understanding. It's a much better and far superior peace, because it doesn't depend on our circumstances going well or making perfect sense.

God is willing to give this peace to us at any time, even at the worst of times. Paul knew this firsthand. As he's writing this letter, Paul is chained in a dark Roman prison facing the very real possibility of a violent execution. He isn't simply sharing encouraging words, Paul is unveiling a secret he has discovered on a very personal level. A wonderful antidote to anxiety.

Paul is saying, in essence, God will give a Perfect Peace to those whose minds are stayed on Him.

Jesus, thank You for showing us a way to live totally free from worry and fear. Thanks for offering Your peace to us at any and every moment of the day. Help me today to catch myself whenever I begin to worry. Help me to turn my worries into prayer reminders and quickly turn these situations over to Your care. I want to experience Your perfect peace. In Jesus' name, Amen.

Day 31
The Devotional Life of Christ

For our last day on this month-long journey, I thought it might be encouraging to reflect a little on the life of Christ. Specifically, on His devotional life, on the way He personally pursued a dependent, one-on-one relationship with the Father.

The reason? The biblical evidence is clear, Jesus enjoyed perfect peace during His time on earth, because He kept His mind stayed on the Father and trusted Him completely. This peace was strengthened and renewed every time He broke away from the crowds, even from His disciples, to draw near to His Father in prayer.

As we read the gospels, there are certainly some things about Jesus we can only marvel at, like the time He walked on water or raised Lazarus from the dead. But other aspects of Christ's life are written down to do more than inspire. Jesus often provided us an example to follow.

That's especially true when we talk about the personal prayer life of Christ.

First, there is the Messianic prophecy in Isaiah that predicts how He would seek the Father every morning: "*The Lord God has given me the tongue of those who are taught* (a disciple), *that I may know how to sustain with a word him who is weary.* **Morning by morning** *He awakens; He awakens my ear to hear as one being taught"* (Isa. 50:4, ESV). The next two verses in this passage make it clear Isaiah is talking about Christ.

I find it interesting that we have no examples of the apostles praying in the gospels. The one time Jesus asked them to pray (in the Garden of Gethsemane on the eve of His death), they fall asleep. But, we see Jesus praying all the time.

In Matt. 6:6, Jesus tells them (and us) how to pray from His own example and practice: *"But when you pray, go into your room and shut your door, and pray to your Father who is in secret. And your Father who sees in secret will reward you."*

In Matt. 14, after hearing of John the Baptist's death, we are told: *"He* (Jesus) *withdrew from there in a boat to a desolate place by himself"* (Vs. 13, ESV). But the crowds interrupted His quiet time. After performing a spectacular miracle, where Jesus fed 5,000 people it says: *"And after He had dismissed the crowds, He went up on the mountain by Himself to pray"* (Vs. 23, ESV).

Mark 1:35 says: *"And rising very early in the morning, while it was still dark, He departed and went out to a desolate place, and there He prayed."* (ESV)

Luke 6:12 says: *"In these days He went out to the mountain to pray, and all night He continued in prayer to God."* (ESV)

Luke 11:1 tells us: *"Now Jesus was praying in a certain*

place, and when He finished, one of His disciples said to Him, 'Lord, teach us to pray…" (ESV)

Even at the end, shortly after the Last Supper, Luke tells us: *"And He came out and went, **as was His custom**, to the Mount of Olives…"* What did He do there? Once again, in the Garden of Gethsemane, Jesus prayed (Luke 22:29-31).

Every day Jesus felt the need to draw near to the Father. It became the Lord's custom all the days of His ministry on earth. If Jesus, the sinless, spotless Son of God needed to connect with the Father like this every day, how much more so do we?

Jesus modeled this level of dependence on the Father, which led Him to live a life of complete obedience, totally free of fear and anxiety. His soul and spirit were constantly replenished through an unbroken abiding in the Lord's presence every day.

Now He extends the same offer to us, to enjoy the gift of Perfect Peace, through the power of the Holy Spirit, as we continue to trust and keep our minds stayed on Him.

Lord Jesus, thank You for opening up the narrow way that leads to life, through Your own obedience and sacrifice. Thank You for offering Your peace and presence to us every day, to help us overcome whatever trials we face. Help us to live each and every day aware of our constant need to stay connected with You. Thank You Holy Spirit that You live within us now, and because You do, we are never, ever alone. In Jesus' name, Amen.

Want to Read More?

Would you like to read more of Dan Walsh's books?

Since 2009, Dan has written over a dozen bestselling novels, mostly for the inspirational and Christian fiction market. All of them are written in a similar style, with character-driven storylines, page-turning suspense and a clean, romantic thread. Most also have a strong spiritual theme or message woven into the story.

If you like reading suspense novels, Dan recommends his novel *When Night Comes*, the first in a new series.

You can get a sneak peek at all of Dan's books or see what others are saying about them, at the link below. Once there, just click on the book cover you're curious about:

http://www.danwalshbooks.com/books/

Want to Help the Author?

If you enjoyed reading this book, the best thing you can do to help Dan is very simple—*tell others about it.* Word-of-mouth is the most powerful marketing tool there is. Better than expensive TV commercials or full-page ads in magazines.

Dan would greatly appreciate it if you would rate his book and leave a brief review at any of the popular online stores (like Amazon), or wherever books are sold.

Even a sentence or two will help.

About The Author

Dan Walsh was born in Philadelphia in 1957. His family moved down to Daytona Beach, Florida in 1965, when his dad began to work with GE on the Apollo space program. That's where Dan grew up.

He married, Cindi, the love of his life in 1976. They have two grown children and three grandchildren. Dan served as a pastor for 25 years, then began writing fiction full-time in 2010. His bestselling novels have won many awards, including 3 ACFW Carol Awards (Book-of-the-Year) and 2 Selah Awards. Three of Dan's novels were finalists for RT Reviews Inspirational Book of the Year.

If you'd like to get an email alert whenever Dan has a new book coming out, or a special deal on one of Dan's books, you can visit his website below and sign up for his newsletter. From his homepage, you can also contact Dan or follow him on Facebook or Twitter.

www.danwalshbooks.com